For my family who have supported and encouraged me on my creative journey.

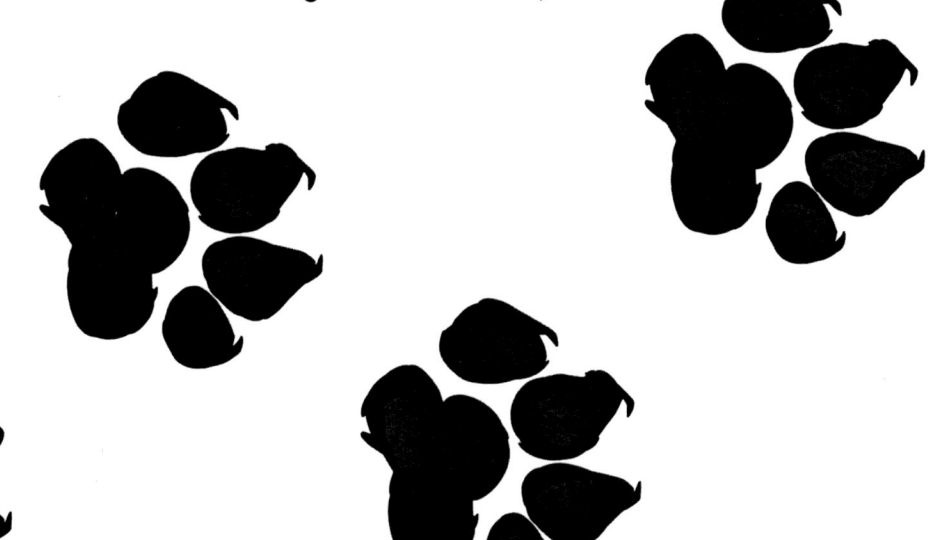

Hank's Backyard Adventure

By:
Rachel Counts

© 2014

Hello! My name is Hank!

It's nice outside. Let's go exploring!

Uh oh! What's that rabbit doing here?
He's not supposed to be here!
I'm going to chase it.

There's that owl again!
He keeps coming back into my yard.
I hope I can catch him today!

Look! It's Walter.
He lives in the pond.
I like to go lie down on the rock
and talk to him.

I hear someone barking! Who is it?

BARK! BARK!

It's Butter, Hank's best friend.
They love to play!

We love to dig together. Look! We found our buried treasure.

We are playing a game of Poker!
Who do you think will win?

I spy a yellow bee!

I spy a purple butterfly!

I spy a red bird!

Look at Butter go!
She is about to catch the ball!

I found a stick. Let's make ourselves a snack!

Can you help me find Butter?

Shh. Don't tell Butter! It's my turn to hide.

Let's go run through the leaves!
It is one of my favorite things to do!

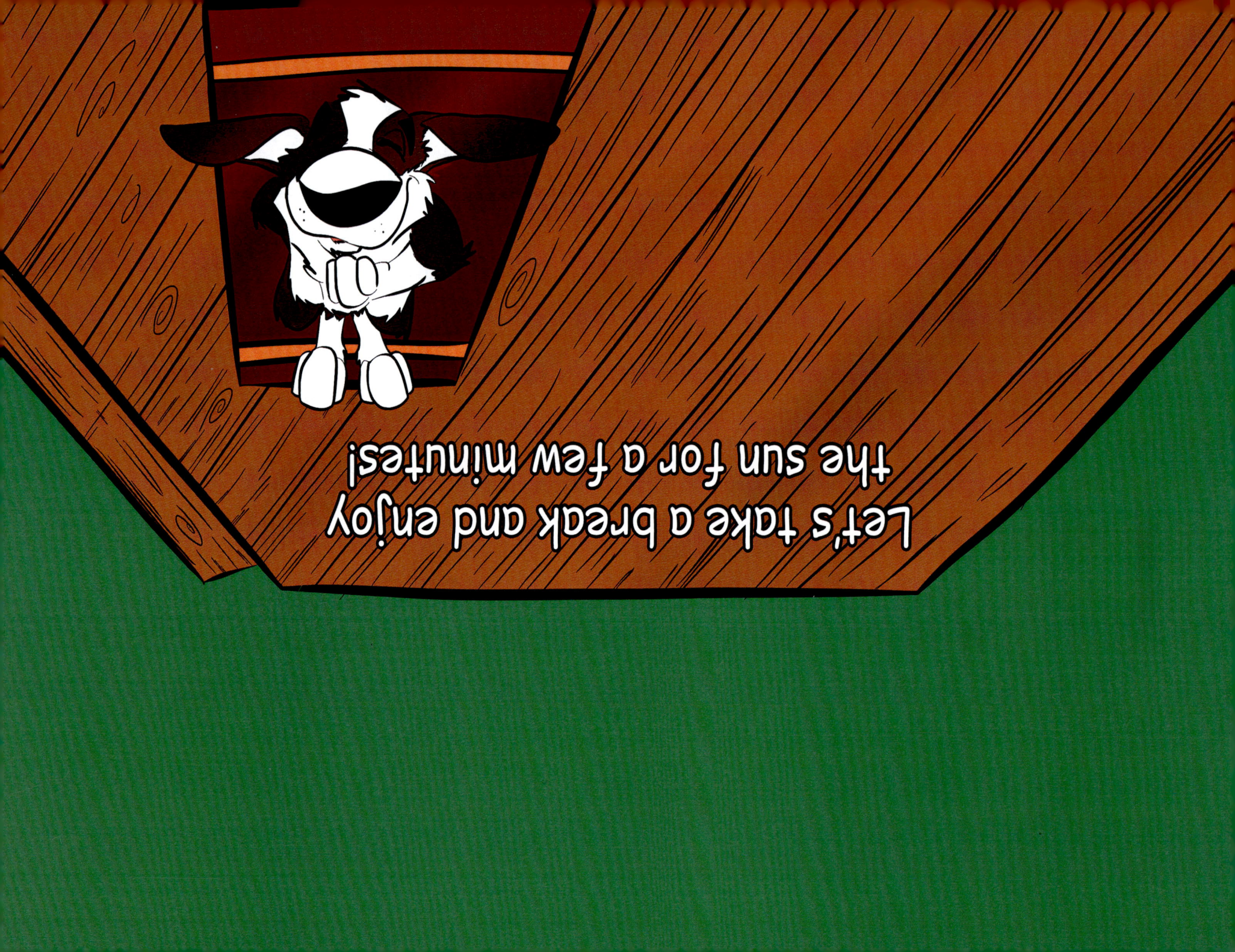

Let's take a break and enjoy the sun for a few minutes!

The sun is going down.
Can you see it over the fence?

Look! There's fireflies everywhere. Butter is about to catch one!

Let's go star gazing!
Can you see the North Star?

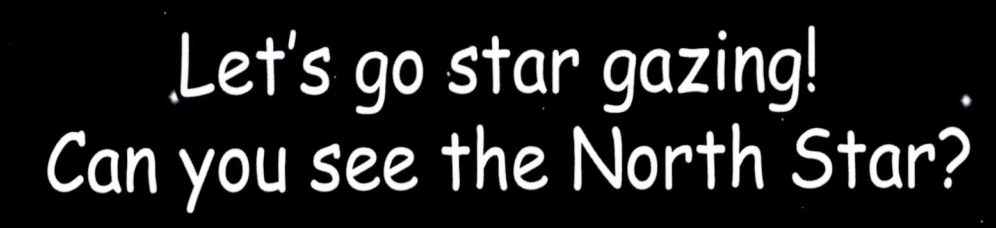

It's getting late.
It's time to go inside.
We are getting tired.

Butter is going home.
Bye Butter!

Good night backyard. See you tomorrow!